# NO HEAVEN

PITT POETRY SERIES
Ed Ochester, Editor

# NO HEAVEN

**ALICIA SUSKIN OSTRIKER**

UNIVERSITY OF PITTSBURGH PRESS

The publication of this book is supported by a
grant from the Pennsylvania Council on the Arts

Published by the University of Pittsburgh Press, Pittsburgh, PA 15260

Manufactured in the United States of America
Printed on acid-free paper
10 9 8 7 6 5 4 3 2 1
ISBN 0-8229-5875-9

*– for JPO*

Imagine there's no heaven,
It's easy if you try,
No hell below us,
Above us only sky,
Imagine all the people . . .

JOHN LENNON

And hard it is in spite of blazoned days.

WALLACE STEVENS

# CONTENTS

III. MATERIAL DENSITY

IV. TEARING THE POEM UP

## CODA

# NO HEAVEN

## VOCATION

*To play among the words like one of them,*
*Lit from within—others can see it,*
*Never oneself—*

She slips like a cat through traffic,
A girl alone downtown
For the first time, subway fare in her purse,

Fear of losing it
Clamping her chest,
Wind whipping tears from her eyes,

Fried grease and gasoline in her nose, shoes and
Jewelry in shopwindows, a spike
Of freedom stitching her scalp—

Though she dreads the allergy shot at the clinic
She feels herself getting brave.
Now it begins to snow on Central Park South

And a flight of pigeons
Whirs up from a small pile of junk in the gutter
Grey, violet, green, a predatory shimmer.

The marquee of the Paris Theater
Looks at the rapturous child
Through downcast lashes, condescendingly.

I watch her over a distance of fifty years.
I see how small she is in her thin coat.
I offer a necklace of tears, orgasms, words.

# I · HERE AND NOW

## BIRDCALL

*—for Elizabeth Bishop*

Tuwee, calls a bird near the house,
Tuwee, cries another, downhill in the woods.
No wind, early September, beeches and pines,

Sumac aflame, tuwee, tuwee, a question and a faint
But definite response, tuwee, tuwee, as if engaged
In a conversation expected to continue all afternoon,

Where is?—I'm here?—an upward inflection in
Query and in response, a genetic libretto rehearsed
Tens of thousands of years beginning to leave its indelible trace,

Clawprint of language, ritual, dense winged seed,
Or as if someone were slowly buttoning a shirt.
I am happy to lie in the grass and listen, as if at the dawn of reason,

To the clear communal command
That is flinging creaturely will into existence,
Designing itself to desire survival,

Liberty, companionship,
Then the bird near me, *my* bird, stops inquiring, while the other
Off in the woods continues calling faintly, but with that upward

Inflection, I'm here, I'm here,
I'm here, here, the call opens a path through boughs still clothed
By foliage, until it sounds like entreaty, like anxiety, like life

Imitating the pivotal move of Whitman's "Out of the Cradle,"
Where the lovebird's futile song to its absent mate teaches the child
Death, which the ocean also whispers—

Death, death, death, it softly whispers,
Like an old crone bending aside over a cradle, Whitman says,
Or like the teapot in Elizabeth Bishop's grandmother's kitchen,

Here at one end of the chain of being,
That whistles a song of presence and departure,
Creating comfort but also calling for tears.

## BUS STATION

Those bus station bathrooms are bad,
You would have to be a desperate
Woman with broken shoe heels
A torn jacket lining
And a child whose face
Has to be washed because the tracks
Of his gritty tears make you ashamed,
To use those bathrooms
With their smell of disinfectant
Like a personal insult

Then you would come out
Not very hopeful, the kid
Unready to control himself,
You would get some candy from a machine
Prop the kid on a bench, wait for the bus
And history to repeat themselves

Outside the revolving doors
Somehow rain would probably be falling
Steadily in slow wet crystal globes
Through the inky night the wet streetlights
The taxis, the entire world.

## CORRESPONDENCE

Two Asian men and a boy keep busy
Fourteen hours a day keeping it open,
The stationery store flanked by the shoe
Shop uptown, the deli downtown, corner
Of Broadway & 112th. You need
A magnifying glass to find this place
Of earnest competence, whose personnel
Sell pens, pencils, paperclips, pads,
Photograph albums, watercolor tubes,
Seven days a week, determined to
Succeed among us big-nosed ghosts on Gold
Mountain. Packed to its beams, the pigmy store
Has everything required for office or
For studio, and the pale assistant can
Locate the customer's precise desire,
Squeezing his minced frame between cupboards
And shelves laden with dusty inventory
Like a man who slips through rain-beaten downtown
Alleys, a step ahead of the secret police.
You work hard, you make money, you get rich—

Or your son does, who becomes a doctor—
If that's not visionary, then what is?

—Here I buy Xerox paper, as intended,
Plus, ah, some envelopes and notepaper,
A dusty teal, fair to the fingertips,
Adventitious! Handmade in Seattle,
The label in non-serif print declares,
By an artisans' co-op over on the far
Side of capitalism, or tucked in one

Of its multitudinous secret pockets,
Where the long wharves stand in quiet mist
That lifts by midday. Now I can write
In-laws, ex-students, dearest friends who thought
Themselves abandoned by me, knowing they'll
Appreciate my word and bond,
As if another age were on its way
In which, with these economies of scale,
Profit to one might mean profit to all,
As if to correspond were capital.

## BROOKLYN TWILIGHT

The man and his son
Walk out into their first American snow
Bundled up and holding hands.

On the corner in front of the baker's
The man tries to pull
His son around, playfully, while

The boy squeals breathlessly
In his Russian accent, *Papa,*
*You're making me fall,*

And softly the neon storefronts
Come on, like a memory
Of prison friendship,

A word of betrayal or rescue,
Causing the flakes to whirl
Rose, camellia, blue,

The length of Pitkin Avenue.

## PICKUP

It is all about speed and flexibility, about speed
And flexibility and teamwork and accuracy. We move
Like neurons charging in your head, man,

Choreography from the ground up,
Meanwhile smelling the hot asphalt and exhaust,
The chain-link fence around the playground spinning

Past the corner of our eye, with the traffic and storefronts,
What the ball feels like in our hands, hard, pebbled, orange
And black, what the dribble feels like,

The sound and pound, the sort of lope we adopt
Getting on and off the court, the way somebody looks
When he starts to play, his face and his sneakers, it's all part of it.

When we swivel it is a whiplash, when we pass it is a cannonball,
When we leap, we hang in the air like Nijinsky taking a nap,
When the ball goes in we slap each others' shoulders and butts

Then turn like a flock of barn swallows, you know our ancestors
Were farmers, they had barns, they watched the birds
Flying around in formation at sunset,

Or a school of fish, you know the way fish dart
In unison, the way the tempo changes and they just bat off?
You can't guess how they do it, you could say

The way we play it, there are no pauses in this game.

## ONE-MINDED

Sitting on waves like a duck you remember the day
At Redondo you got addicted, just watching
What you instantly recognized as joy—

It was some surfer on a seven-foot stick
Riding the water's beautiful beachward shrug
Hanging five, floating, and you meant
To be that boy,
So you started young
Playing hooky, bouncing on your short board
Learning from the local older guys, and you can still
Hear yourself squeal-yell taking your first drop
Into a bottom-turn, then it was easy and
Blacker than orgasm
Blacker than a single person's orgasm
Hunting beauty and terror like warriors
With your buddies down the world's collapsing edges
Every summer, mad for the splash of endorphins—

Rocking on water you remember meeting eternity
Inside a spinning lime-green funnel, hey,
There it finally was, and there
You were, and then spit
Out of the time hole, riding over the lip—

You go on into your fifties, erect,
You surf until your face reflects
A solitary blankness like sainthood
But you never even think about your face,
You're thinking there's just one brotherhood
And only one pure rhythm, paddling

Out on your stomach
Waiting for the outer wave
Catching it, standing and riding home

Now you're hoping to die in your wet suit
And if death could capture you
On a day like this,
The swells
Sheer glass, the air
Unbelievably mild, balmy—
If he'd clasp you to his heart
And pitch you into the ocean, that brainless grave
Today, today you'd be superbly glad.

## LIKING IT

Some men like it if the woman can't tell
Whether it's a gun she has in her mouth
Or a prick.

Some women believe the shallow razor slashes
Their lovers make on their necks
(Underneath the long

Elliptically tangled hair) and chest
Are like a secret engagement dramatized by a real
Diamond, to be proud of

But not reveal. He's her high school
Mathematics teacher, and she does it to him, too,
Because after the vodka comes the need to punish

Their sinful bodies, she thinks about it all week,
Bright red released in lines like devil's writing coming out,
The sharing of blood, the licking, the cleansing

Of wounds, and how perfectly painful that is,
Cuts even hiss from the alcohol swab, it's like acid,
And the candles in the living room dance like they're alive,

Like hellfire, you can't imagine
The discipline required. The purity
Of self-loathing needed to cut the man

You love—what do her parents understand about love,
She wonders, her poor parents not guessing
What her arms look like under her sleeves:

White nicks, white nicks, white crucifixes,
Sharp little mouse tracks up and down. Some men
Like you to wear a religious medal

When you fuck, some women
Like the man to cry and beg forgiveness.

## CROSSTOWN

Back in New York I grab a taxi at Port Authority,
A young Jamaican guy, then a big Af-Am guy in
A monster silver SUV tries to cut him off but he dashes
Round in front like a fox and then can't move
So we're sitting in the traffic people leaning
On their horns all around us and the big guy comes
Out and starts threatening my driver —*I'm just out
Of jail.* —*So go back to jail.* No love lost it happens
All the time, *They think they are tough and we are
Nothing, we think they are worse than nothing.*
He's been driving two years saving to go to school
To catch up on his computer design skills, the wife
Got impatient and cheated on him, he still sees his
Little daughter who is so pretty and smart she can
Read at the age of four. He'd like to be a better
Christian but working this job he gets in situations
Where he uses bad language. Next day another
Cabbie this one older we talk about Iraq and about power
I say we are seeing the defects of democracy
He says he doesn't believe in democracy democracy
Is for the rich.

Went to Sheila's, we walked on Riverside Drive as
The sun was setting bathing the high limbs of the elms
Coral, the trunks sinking into darkness, we were
Happy together and other walkers also looked happy
Trees tranquilly surviving blight seemed fine
A man passed us with a poodle so elegant it looked
Like a model on a runway.

Small kid on the crosstown bus, a high clear voice:
*If you kick somebody, people won't be your friend.*
Woman next to me carries a large flat manila envelope
Her makeup is violent her middle-aged hair is lacquered
Her coat olive green embroidered cashmere expensive
I think art? photography? then I see the envelope says
X-rays, so it's cancer.

## CIGARETTES

In Chester, Mass., a morning after rain,
Walking along Rte. 20, back from town,
I notice near the curb an empty
Soft-pack of Camels: conspicuous
Against the roadway's clean unmottled tar,
Light as a crab's discarded husk,
One of the men rebuilding
The old Post Office must have cast it here.

Makes me recall the enchanting nicotine scent
Clinging to teenage packs of Luckies
I'd stick my nose in after removing the last
Cigarette, before I threw the pack away
Together with its dim shimmer of foil—
Palm-sized caves of paper and magic.
It had to be Luckies to show my loyalty
To Mary and Cathy, who smoked brazenly
In the playground where the nuns could see.

Ten years later it was Marlboros,
Some rungs higher on the social ladder,
Hard packs that wouldn't get crushed in my purse.
There was filtering going on, and somehow less
Fragrance in the empty boxes, but smoking
And even bumming smokes was something good
And wicked to do with my hands and mouth.
A person needed that sense of freedom and risk
And had a right to it. Those were the sixties
And if I was not on the barricades
Or dropping acid with my students—well,
Year after year I was Lauren Bacall

Tossing her hair back over her shoulder
Then dragging hard, then looking at the man.
What did I see if I looked at myself?
Wife, mother, teacher, daughter,
Identities like matching sheets and blankets
To tuck a person safely in at night
And keep her dreamless. No wonder I liked
That air of glamour in my little life,
That suicide, that option.

Decades now since I quit, and decades since
I surrendered to safety belts. And I like to walk, but still,
Too much goodness is bad. Hitting the road
Toward our cabin, the kids, the grandkids, I thank the Lord
There is still alcohol.

## IN THE FORTY-FIFTH YEAR OF MARRIAGE

*—for JPO*

I would never say I feel like a million dollars, but I whistle
While I work, I'm rounding the curve, and I've had ecstasies
And anguishes, so I'm ready for something else.

Sometimes I feel like a trucker, living this American life,
*He doesn't care if it rains or freezes, long as he's got his plastic Jesus,*
High in the cab and moving fast but lonely,

Sometimes I feel like a mailman who faithfully visits each door in his
    district,
Sometimes like a mermaid out of water. Often like a blind woman
Who sits and waits in the dark, but sometimes

Honey, when I imagine your face
All my quiescent emotions leap to the image
Like children when a father returns from a trip—

He looks tired, he hasn't put down his bags yet
And his tie is skewed, but the middle sister gives him a big hug, the older
Kisses him on both cheeks, the younger one drags on his pant leg

And soon will be whining, their little brother sits like a Buddha
Blissfully gazing at him. Only their mother
Doesn't leave the kitchen. She's fixing dinner. Anything wrong, he asks

And she says no. Sometimes when we're talking I dwell on how
Appealing your face has become, since you've grown old,
Its shapeliness less eighteenth century, less rounded and resisting,

More nineteenth century expressive, more Rodin, more Thomas Eakins,
Many mobile surfaces to it, the brow and the skin around the eyes
Especially finely molded, the lips more supple and kind.

The legs are another thing my eye favors, the hands also, can they
Have grown more shapely, more like Rembrandt? It seems so. Of smells
And tactilities between us I need say nothing, you know all

There is to know, and of the sorrow, anger and jealousy in the pantry
Sitting uselessly on the shelf for decades, the woman won't
Throw them out but she's never found a recipe that uses them.

Marriage is that complicated, a house with living rooms and bedrooms,
And the usual basement and attic nobody likes to go to—
Horrible cobwebs in the basement, low rafters in the attic—

It is tough, that cord not easily broken
That sometimes seems a noose, but today I wished to speak
Of your beauty, bravely cresting in your sixties, at an age

When your parents were gone, an attractive hard-living
Man and woman, and perhaps they've lent your clay
This extra splendor for me to appreciate

—*That I'll have to leave ere long. As time goes by. Silver threads among,*
*For it's a long long way. Each precious day.* I'm reading Ecclesiastes
And the eye is not filled with seeing.

## RUNNING OUT THE CLOCK

—*for JPO*

When we started living together we used to sit at a wooden table
Side by side studying, touching each other between the legs,
Remember, and in a sense we have gone on doing that.

We carry each other's minds everywhere for safekeeping,
Our bodies bear traces of each other's bodies,
Surface and depth, when you are absent I sleep on your side of the bed.

You made me laugh, I made you be serious, we taught each other
*Whatsoever thy hand findeth to do, do it with thy might*
And many other pieces of ancient wit,

Thereby hung a tale, our tales, our tails, we worked our asses off
And played as hard as we could, not to waste the time that on earth
Was given us, to live as our parents living and dead would approve,

To raise the children healthy and smart, and good and free,
To earn respect and love, though it is not polite to say it,
As much love as we could possibly—

Arriving at what should be the age of wisdom we keep very busy,
You say what we're doing is running out the clock
As if we could stop the other team from beating us,

Or erase our mistakes. I say I feel the undertow,
Some water still pushing in, breaking in a lively froth, but also
The seductive pull outward, downward, not especially cold or frightening,

More a call from afar, *Let go, little boat, let go, you can swim,*
Whatever else we're doing, wherever we are, we are having this
    conversation—
After living so many years with the din of duty and of ego

If it is time to give them a rest, we wonder what will follow.
We are almost ready. Whether we sit at table or lie warmly in bed,
What we feel in the deep heart's core is a little afraid,

A little set for adventure, getting ready to go.
*I go where I love and where I am loved,* said H.D.
When she was old, *Into the snow.*

## WILDERNESS

—*for JPO*

We left the roadway and climbed up the trail
On past the basalt field, and it was rocky,
Behind us loomed a long extinct volcano,

Joshua trees ruled the landscape, the booklet said
They were so named by the Mormons because their bizarre
Limbs looked like arms flung in desperate prayer.

The dead tea-colored fronds covered their trunks clumsily
Like John the Baptist's haircloth. There was a yellow lizard,
The berries of the juniper were frosted blue,

There were no other people, no birds, and after the abandoned
Mine and a series of ridges with views over Lost Horse Valley
The trail was rougher, disappeared, you could feel the loneliness

Of the earth. The earth wasn't sure
If it wanted people to disturb its vast repose, it already had
Other living beings. Around us to the horizon it rolled

Its big rude stony beauty. We sat on stones and ate our sandwiches.
We were high, we hiked. The last four miles followed a streambed
Flat and sandy as a beach, shrubbery above our heads,

We were tribeless, it was only the two of us
On one of the stretches of our journey
That make us happy the way a child is happy

When it's allowed to be naked, and the meeting
Of all that bare skin with air, blue air, a little breeze,
Makes it jump with joy on the family grass.

## THE SPEECH OF THE CREATURE

*—for Abigail*

The night before you were born
I was sitting on a Berkeley floor drinking wine,
Playing a game of Scrabble with the ones
Who soon were going to be your parents
And losing badly, but before I went to bed
I told them to wake me if anything happened.

In the morning the March light woke me
Flying through the eucalyptus
And the square windowpanes onto my quilt
And onto the varnished hardwood floor.
It was quiet in the house. Not a sound.
Out the window a cat was strolling the sidewalk.

The other bedroom was empty, also full of sunlight
And dancing dust, the furniture stood quietly
Amid this emptiness that cannot be described,
It is so full of loss and of great space together,
Pain and happiness together. While I waited for the call
From the hospital, you were leaving your tight wet world

Forever, and as you know, a young woman scientist
And a young policy wonk—two serious people
Who had lived whole lives without you,
Did problem sets, read books, played ultimate Frisbee —
Were metamorphosing into your mom and dad.
Soon they were confused and new,

Excited as if they had twinned themselves
The way you're a different person with the dolls

That are your children, except they didn't want to boss you—
To them you were like ice cream,
To them you were the most precious pearl,
You were like the wildest magic in Harry Potter.

The third night of your life
When you couldn't sleep, I walked you for an hour
Bouncing your small weight on my shoulder
Sniffing your fragrant scalp, feeling where your
Skimpy bottom was, your slender feet, your limp back
Inside the yellow blanket like a puppy.

They played Beatles and Mozart your first week,
Stubble grew on your father's chin,
Your mother's breasts were huge and leaky,
You were the size of a large cat
And they cherished you so much it made me cry,
Wishing every child born on the planet could have that

Kind of love. I remember a sink full of dishes I was washing.
Swaying with exhaustion your sweet dad was keeping me company.
Suddenly he frowned and said, *If anybody touches my daughter,*
*I'll kill him.* Both our jaws dropped, both of us laughed
At what came out of his mouth,
The speech of the creature.

## WHAT YOU CANNOT REMEMBER,
## WHAT YOU CANNOT KNOW

*—for Abigail*

When you were two you used to say
*I can do it all by myself,* then when you were three
You had tantrums, essentially
Because you wanted to go back and be a baby like before,
And also to be a grownup.
It was perplexing,
It was a mini-rehearsal
For adolescence, which lurks inside your body
Now that you are almost nine,
Like a duplicate baby, an angel
Or alien, we don't know which,
Forceful and intelligent and weird,
Playing with the controls.
Fetal eyes blinking, non-negotiable demands
Like Coke bubbles overflowing a glass,
It strengthens and grows.
When you read it stares through your eyes,
It vibrates when you practice piano,
The cotton dresses hang in your closet
Like conspirators, wavering in its breeze.
We watch you turn inward, your hair
Falls over your face like a veil that hides whatever
You would rather others don't know,
You lean your head listening
For its keen highstrung melancholy voice.
Here comes the gypsy caravan,
Ding-a-ling, the icecream man,
Plenty of glee and woe up the road.
We would do anything for you,
Sweetie, but we can do nothing—
You have to do it all by yourself.

## MAY RAIN, PRINCETON

Green, green, the luminous maples preen,
Swaying like girls at a prom
Waiting to be asked to dance,

The bird feeders need daily refilling, the hot
Azaleas enhance their orange and fuchsia tints,
The rhododendrons puckered dryly inside

Their big buds have begun to force themselves out,
Apple blossoms lie in shallow pools
At the feet of their trunks. All afternoon

Relentless pouring rain soaks the ground,
Beats the roofs, rat-tat,
Races down the gutters.

I imagine it falling into the Hudson River
Around the scows and barges. I imagine it
Splashing the yellow slickers of road crews.

I pretend that I am farms and towns stretched out
The breadth of New Jersey and Pennsylvania
Flat on my back looking up at a gray sky.

The grays shift, it must be windy up there,
I feel the rain batter me, how good it is, cleansing
The air, pocking my skin—

Good, good, like sex after childbirth
When the body is keen
For pleasure again.

## BABY CARRIAGES

In the photograph there are two of them, and a stroller.
The women sit on a bench, wearing their usual day clothes,
That thin stooped one wears a flowered rayon dress,

This one has dark lipstick on, a third is older and has a perm.
The women look relaxed, like people who have known each other forever.
Later they'll feed their babies, then do the laundry or go shopping.

I don't see the babies but I feel their presence
Like invisible magnets that keep the photograph from falling apart,
The animal premise of the whole image.

Behind the bench is a strip of garden and a brick wall
The shadowless sun is bathing. The carriages themselves are funny,
High off the ground and shaped and lacquered like the coaches of royalty.

The date of the photograph is 1942. Wartime, the home front,
It makes sense, I stand in front of it on the museum wall
For a long time, thinking: Here's the real story. If only.

## WHAT IS NEEDED AFTER FOOD

The darkness doesn't war against the light,
It carries us forward
to another light. . . .

In my land, called holy,
they won't let eternity be:
they've divided it into little religions,
zoned it for God-zones,
broken it into fragments of history,
sharp and wounding unto death.

—YEHUDA AMICHAI

*—for Linda Zisquit*

And so beautiful it cracks the bones, especially Jerusalem
With the lustre of her stones, the hurt in her eyes,
And our dreams for her children: a triangle,

Beauty, despair, hope . . . the whole *mishpochah*
Pulling three ways at the same time
Like the people in so many families,

Fighting but joined at the hip, or call it a sandwich,
Despair the filling embraced by the bread of beauty and hope,
Like a manna we eat every day, sent from above,

While on earth in Jerusalem my friend's husband and son
Relax from a sabbath meal, like well-fed beasts,
Happily slumped watching the aftermath

Of a game where the Nazareth team has just won
And vaulted from the bottom of their league
To the top, the players have stripped off their shirts,

Hugging and dancing, circle dancing, belly dancing,
Waving at crowds in the stands to make them cheer louder.
The coach strips his shirt from his hairy barrel chest,

Climbs a wire fence, wobbles and waves his hips.
When someone asks how he feels about his team
(A mix of Jews, Moslems, and one Nigerian,

He himself is Druze), he punches the air
And roars, *I beat them all! I beat Arafat! I beat Sharon!*
*I show them we love each other!* We watch a while,

The celebration is still going on when we quit
To go back to the kitchen, where loaves of beauty and hope
Stand on the counter and the cup of despair goes on the shelf,

My friend and I, we don't ask for much, we read Amichai,
We're not messianic, we don't expect utopia, which is anyway
Another name for a smiling prison,

But love is a good idea, we think, why on earth not.
Simple women that we are, simple mothers cleaning up
The kitchen after one meal to make it ready for the next.

## CITY THROUGH WHICH TIME RUSHES LIKE WATER

All over the new Berlin the museums are like gigantic white
Glistening pearls among reefs, and like divers lured by a deep
Undersea mystery, hypnotized, we swim from one to the next
Breathing through our masks. Unified . . . what can it mean to be unified . . .

Down here the birdlike inscriptions to Innana
Twitter to us, dignified Babylonian griffins
Parade along the sea-green lacquered tiles
Of the Gate of Ishtar in the Pergamon,

The heads of Nefertiti and her shockingly
Complex-faced mother-in-law in the Egyptian Museum
Stare at the far end of the Schlosstrasse bus line, we go on
To the portraits of Glückel and Herzl in Liebeskind's Jewish Museum

With its tunnels and games. An enormous past lies in these marble hands,
Of course it is a stolen past, reminding us that every past
Must be torn from a pit of forgetfulness, a conquest
That makes it precious, while in outer air

Constructions climb overhead everywhere
Like dramatic scenes from Hebrew and Greek creation myths,
As if starting from scratch were possible and necessary,
A heroic hope, and all the while we recognize

We are not Berliners, we are tourists with cameras,
So we turn to the graffiti, the art of the present
Splashed with the fury of animals, of escaped prisoners
Who remember beatings and torture, an orgy of painting

On chopped chunks of the Wall, on peeling residences
Scheduled for demolition, oh the present
Which we stand and photograph is fiercely alive,
If doomed like everything else to disappear

As waves of time beat against cliffs of loss . . .
Baghdad was Babylon, Istanbul was Byzantium,
The city is only a channel . . .

Another cracked world trying to heal itself
Calls on its inner forces . . .

Distant in time and space as forgiveness . . .

## POEM BEGINNING WITH A LINE BY RUMI

*—for Tess O'Dwyer*

*Only those who have felt the knife can understand the wound*
And all the same there are days when to walk a city
—New York, London, Prague—is like feeling completely healed,

With satisfying presents raining down, sheets and squares
Of window glass, countless apartment and car windows,
Store windows, objects to buy,

Pebbled traffic lights flipping from red to green
Penetrating your eyes like a gaze. Buses and taxis,
Signs and symbols, food, stone on stone

Churches, garbage, clothing and hats,
Steam puffing from grates,
Heels striking sidewalk,

Rectangles between buildings a sharp blue on the best days,
Even playgrounds and verdant parks, and park benches
And wineglass elms, spots of complete happiness

And pride, salary that you haven't earned.
Confess there exist days when you want to do nothing
But walk for miles of streets, not buying but looking,

Looking and blessing, and if they give you a river
To remind you still more fully of death and life,
You'll note the ferries, the laboring barges, the bridges

And the speedboats. A material density
Whipped by energy. Here in the windy bay
A boatload of fishermen, maybe Italian,

Efficiently heave up ponderous netfuls
Of squirming bream together with eels,
Nipples and phalluses streaming

From the brine and now the sun is
Descending burning orange, the flaming
Blankets of clouds gathering to swallow it.

Your chest leans against a railing,
Your eyes are like arms pulling the sensations in,
Your heart is completely pierced.

The orange sun lights the indifferent waves,
The wooden boat rocks, surrounded by ocean,
All is in fact natural calm and passionless

Except the tugging sailors, the frantic fish—

*O always moving brine upon which we ride*
*O setting tremendous sun*
*O stinging cold*
*O edge of city*
*O slapping water and spume caught by the air.*

# II · ARCHIVAL

PREVIOUSLY UNCOLLECTED POEMS,
1975–1995

## NORMAL LIGHT

Normal light never killed anything.
When I beam my affection at you
Do not duck. It is not bullets.
Do not try to impersonate Superman.
It is not Kryptonite.

What normal light wishes and dreams about
During its flight is how it will encounter
An object: every photon imagines this
The way we imagine gateways, that slowly open
As we fly toward them, into gardens,

The poppies and peonies making their mouths wide.
What actually happens to the light:
Striking a surface, some particles rebound
And keep going, some are absorbed
And become heat, that's it.

That's usually it. But some
Flash on and inward to the curious cave
That is light's garden, light's antithesis,
And form an image.

                    Sometimes an object struck
Where it has eyes, will see.
                           Light dreams of this.

## LETTER OF INQUIRY

*—for Diana Hume George*

When others and especially the young
Do it better than I, do with ease
What requires unbelievable labor
And persistence through despair on my part,
When I watch the young make free with art
And love, and God, they are so attractive
About their pure physicality and energy,
Their headbands and shades and jeans,
Their decent untouchable T-shirted ribcages,
Their high-hat way with an American
Vocabulary and set of cadences
And premises I'd give an arm for,
I have to want to kill myself sometimes—

Yet I don't give it up. Why not?
Diana, when the hammer of fifty hit me
Like a thing on auction that was going cheap,
When I looked up the road and saw
That eerie fog-bank, a formless future,
The back of somebody's van with the army blankets,
Those tubes, those needles, those paralyzed years,

What was it you told me, that helped?
You put aside a moment, didn't you,
The chart of your distress. You said:
*Do I have to draw you a picture?*
You drew me a map, and marked it
*Here.* And *here.* Like the good passages
In somebody else's biography,
Somebody in for the stretch—Blake or H.D.—

One of our dotty heroes who never quit.
You trusted me enough to laugh at me.

You shut the door, didn't you, a moment,
On your own squalling, nosebleeding woes,
To reassure me, not that you were there,
But that I was. Dear,
I'm still not ready for gardening
Or politics or charity.
Poetry and love are what I know.
They made me glad, and now they worry me.
*Over and done,* I mutter. *Over and done.*
Diana, what did you say? Would you say it again?

## HE GETS DEPRESSED WHENEVER WE ARGUE

Man, I am talking to you
In my secret woman voice
And I would like it to feel
Like something from the inside of your head.

I am emitting this message today
While I walk home a half a snowy mile
Kicking the slush
And the shovelled boulder sized lumps
That lie in my path.
Places where nobody has cleared the sidewalk
I climb over the snowplowed ridges
And walk in the gutter in the twilight. Can you
Hear me? You are of course in Los Angeles,
Land of the cowboy and Indian, busy
At a conference. It never snows there
But we have been married so many years
I imagine you hear me perfectly well. Listen,
You Jeremiah, you lamenting
Son of the father, what
Will your mama think of your behavior,
This childish
Sullenness before you left. Listen,
Don't you ever say to yourself
This woman is my woman now forever,
A lifelong proposition, because I like her,
Because she suits me, drinking wine,
Taking a bath, talking,
The mentality suits me, the body
Given me plenty of satisfaction
Over the years and more to come.

I mean lifelong
Lifelong
Think about it, lifelong
What a sweet and pretty sound
If you think about it right.

A sound like *treasure*
A sound like *precious*
I mean it has that trochee lilt
That dying fall.
What I mean is don't you sometimes say
Well, hallelujah, it's the whole damn package
Better grab it, grasp it
Like a kite in your windy mind,
Like a kite tugging and diving,
Or like the decision you made
Far back, far back
To be born in the first place,
To seize the whirling opportunity
Of life no matter what
And believe me
This is always a choice
Made in ignorance
And courage. Same, honey,
With the person you love, when finally
The light comes on and you realize it's forever,
It's the whole package with the strings attached,
Might as well love it kicking and scratching
While hating it
While of course trying to tie it down
Secretly hope it keeps its craziness

Its freedom that you first married it for,
Its own strange and unfinished life.

Of course I'm speaking from the experience
Of riding you,
Honey, like a wild and bucking horse
In some western movie
Quite a while now,
You streaking across the prairie
Me hanging on the bridle
Laughing and crying
And singing hallelujah
Fit to die.

My boots squeak on the snow as darkness falls,
The night is going to be clear here
In New Jersey,
The stars are going to come out
Like pinpricks,
The air will be big and pure, a pleasure to breathe.
Please get in touch:
I need to know how it is in California.

## THE IDEA OF MAKING LOVE

The idea of making love     as sticking your tongue
into the calyx of the other          & licking up
its nectar     while being licked yourself        we
like this         because we are always manufacturing
nectar     and when someone sticks a pointy tongue
into us and takes a drop     on the tongue-tip and
swallows it     we make more nectar     we can always
     make more          of our own nectar and
        are always thirsty for the nectar of others

# ANOTHER IMAGINARY VOYAGE

*—for K.J.*

When kabbalists declare
Each deed we do affects
Beings in other worlds,
My thought turns round to sex,

As it inclines to do,
As needle to true north,
Considering our case,
Weighing it back and forth.

What if we had undressed
That chaste July, and what
If we were being watched
Or watched *for,* as a boat

Reported missing brings
A crowd down to the shore,
To wager whether it
Will or will not appear,

The fog so thick, the sea
Invisible, until
A form coagulates,
And someone calls, "A sail!"

And all things clear. To you,
No comfort; you would see
Yourself step from the deck
Straight into custody;

There follows a swift trial,
A sentence swift and crude
(Reflecting guilt and fear)
To penal servitude.

While I—I can't agree
Touch is a sin, and so
I picture a small crowd
Of sleepless townsfolk who

Have waited out the night
And stand at crimson dawn
Ready to welcome us
With garlands and with wine.

To tell if I am right,
Or you, all books are dumb;
This is among the secrets
Kept by the world to come.

## EXTENDED SONNET

Love is not love that likes another's pain
Or its own suffering either. It has a sweet
Tooth but for merriment, the chapel stone
Of love feels cool and smooth to naked feet
That walk around in it under the moon
And curl together listening to owls
Call and call. They giggle in
Their cupped palms, for they are only children—
This ruin has no roof, it is so old,
The midnight wind is full of oranges.
*Kennst du das land?*
                                    Past the hedgerow a hill
Flattens out to the field of father's hand
Where we trotted and sniffed, before the furrows turned
To a checkbook and shot glass,
Before it bit its nails to the cuticle—
Love could revoke our exile from that ground.

## MISERY AND FRUSTRATION

*—for M.S.*

They say one part of wisdom
Is learning to let go when you have to.
But if you give up your good drinking buddies
Misery and frustration, you wonder
What else might drop from the picture.
There is this problem with recovery
You'd like to mention to your counselor,
If you could find the right moment, because
The group somehow doesn't seem to touch it.
Will your sex life go blank like a movie screen
After the feature, your brain
Lapse from keen, your art depart
Like Antony's gods? Surely a man should worry?
Then there's the issue of brutality.
You hate to be mean. Misery and frustration
Were loyal pals for years; don't you owe them?

Yes, but remember your gardening arts and skills
Have taught you how to be kind to tendrils.
Unwind them cautiously. You can tell
They're living things by their tensile grip.
What you can't tell is that they're parasites,
Thieves and killers. Well, that's nature for you—
Every organism for itself.

Do not burn them.
Carry them off to the forest,
Which will slowly eat them.
Misery and frustration are delicious,
They'll make good mulch, you'll see them join

What Wordsworth called the life of things,
Those porous layers, though it may take years.
Meanwhile invent a ritual farewell.
In the men's sweat house one unstated aim
Is to extrude the bitter juice of grief
While gravely regarding one's own genitals
And watching others too, scanning their scars,
Until the heat becomes intolerable
And the heart threatens to stop.
I know a woman who buried her uterus
After her hysterectomy, and said prayers for it,
Although rabbis advised her this would be lawless.
At least you've learned to cry, at least there's that.
Meanwhile—look at your hands
Starting to sprout.

They say another part of wisdom
Is opening, letting things enter, making welcome
As to festival—come on, unbutton here, unloose the stubborn
Doors from their jambs—
But that's a knowledge you already know.

## MID-FEBRUARY

*—for Maxine Kumin*

The mare rears, she has almost thrown her rider.
It's the thaw, it's the scent of spring,
The animals know it before we do.
While the lot of us shiver and fret
Over the ozone layer and the whale,
Incorrigibly peering forward and backward
In the manner of our species,
New Hampshire is a patient who seems to heal,
Left to herself. See how she kicks at her blanket.

Inside here, the windows are steaming up
But a path runs through the woods,
Half dirty snow, half mud
With the stones sticking through
And the snapped branches lying across, the ones
That were ready to die
And gave themselves to the wind.
Friend, it's a day for a walk.
Are we going to walk it?

## COASTAL DAWN

*—for S.P.*

Over a dune between summer cottages
Air still a little chill but the wind soft
Three deer drift toward the sea:
A six-point buck, a doe, a spotted fawn.
The buck skitters at the foam—
Shall I, shan't I—
His family watches, I watch.
He cannot make himself enter the water.
It is calm, the breakers are tiny
And it is almost the end of August.

You think August will last forever?
No, no, it can't.

You think what you feel for me can last?
A spark ignites and bulges on the horizon.
The buck concludes that the sea is unimportant.
The deer race away like vapor,
A hot ordinary day begins

To stroke my forehead and knees.

III · MATERIAL DENSITY

## WOODEN VIRGIN WITH CHILD

Once the trunk of a lovely tree
She sits on her narrow chair
In an alcove of the Cloisters.
Patient, modestly shawled,
As yet only slightly hunched,
For she is still young, in fact
(Though dry, cracked a bit
Flecks of paint clinging to bodice)
Like one fresh from the convent.
Selfless, she does what she's told
But will not meet your eye.
The manchild between her knees like a doll,
Hand risen to bless, but headless,
Is the one with the book.

You and I stand and look
In our velvet jackets and tough
Boots, free to come or go,
At this mystery. Who
Would have been the model, was she
The sculptor's mother, was she his wife?
Honor his wisdom, to know
That God needs the protection
Of this sad, simple woman,

His wish also to pity her, she
Who is said to be the incarnation of pity.

## THE KISS OF JUDAS

Among many, one panel:
Perhaps it catches the eye
Due to its symmetry
Or its subject, betrayal.

Giotto is simple.
What does "simple" mean?
Soldiers, torches, a friendship,
Money, a kiss.

Two profiles: one looks upward,
Lips protrude with intention,
Brow slightly frowns.
And one receptive, brunette,

Eyes almost Byzantine,
Grave if not solemn,
His neck remains bare
To show absence of fear.

Judas wears a cloak
To reveal that he's hidden.
His embrace also hides
The other man's body.

Could Judas wish to become
Joined with his Lord's body?
Giotto has painted him
Like almost everyone else

In the Scrovegni Chapel,
Slightly rounded, short,
Not too far from being
A dog or a bird.

Isn't it hard, though, to leave?
Pope Leo liked them. We too,
Those tender Giotto blues,
Those rose tints, those ash-greens.

We were never in a church
More comforting than this one.
Imagine if women's wombs
Had paintings like this one.

All of us would be born
Wise and good, then.

## THE BIRTH OF VENUS

**I**

Huge shell the remnant of my great-grandmother dragon,
Split open to form the world,
They have made a boat of it
And set me here.

The effect is of scarcely tolerable pleasure.

**II**

If I am anything I am young, so young.
As I arrive on this shallow scalloped sea
Zephyr huffs flowers at me, frowning.
The effect is to deepen my reverie.

My face emerges from another world
Behind the picture plane, a world
Of light and clouds, volumes of clouds.
The artist has set it at an impossible angle

Upon my impossibly swanlike
Neck, my impossibly sloping shoulders.

If I am anything I am unreal.

**III**

All this is genius: the patchy blues of sky
Filled in behind me, the sensitive penciling of the hand
With which I touch myself, contrasted with the crudely dashed
Bronze accents on foliage to my left, wings to my right,

Same gorgeous color as my hair, a wheat
That might nourish a province, and, where a shoulder's edge
Meets a pale background, traces of draughtsmanship
Reveal revision, which is a kindness, or an insolence . . .

Or a looseness beyond perfection.

IV

My knees together, slightly inturned . . .

My rosy foot, with a peasant's long capable toes . . .

A woman steps from the forest.
She looks Roman, a matron under orders
To wrap me in patterned cloth.
I myself am Greek and do not see her.

V

Hair uncoiling in breeze,
Oval belly, petite globular breasts,
And the great shell

Imply a categorical
Encyclopedia of curves,
A Euclidean feast.

Scallops imply an open universe
Like the bit of open sea
At the back of the canvas.

## VI

I am a factory of flowers. Lilies without, roses within,
I will be loved, the hunters will shoot me,
The gardeners pluck me, I must fade, I must die

To assume an immortal order,
You must write about me. Unforgettable,
That is what I am, and I must die

To be remembered, I must reappear
As April garden plots, moist outdoor earth
Delved and planted around a hothouse, a navel.

## VII

The navel, smallest of circles, at the latitude of the horizon,
Echoed by nipples.

## VIII

At times I dream I am a warrior,
At times a revolutionary.
Can this account for my glazed-ceramic look,
A girl's chaste fantasy?

Between the dreams and myself lie two chasms of time.
I carry neither spear nor gun

Circle after circle, history after history.
Would you say that I am wistful, ineffably melancholy,
That I appear to ask pardon for my beauty?

## IX

Now that I am here I will proliferate.
I will be poorly copied
But I will not object

(I object to nothing, I have no complaint).
For the next six centuries girls will pose like this
To represent innocence, trailing one foot.

But I am neither love nor innocence,
I am only exquisite.
Nobody is ever loved enough,

Our mothers say. I am less than skin deep,
No deeper than canvas, an undercoat
and these thin areas of gilt, sapphire, white.

## X

It is one thing to gaze, from the self's jail, at things.
Another to *be* a thing, an entity.
Lastly, to fuse the two, be the self's self. The soul
At once all-seeing and utterly blank, meaningless

As a cloud or river.

Now look at my eyes. Be pitiless,
Use me as your mirror.

## XI

Before my birth you were an animal,
Or supposed yourself one.
You lived among the pigs in mud and straw
Having forgotten almost everything

Pertaining to the gods.

Before my birth, confess it, you were savage.
Seeing me now you forsake your appetites,
Drawn by the gentle half-lit tenderness
Of my inward gaze,

Subtly indented nostrils, coral lips,
The weightless gravity of my porcelain face,
The contemplative ivory of my form, my air of trust—

## XII

The limousine that dropped me on your street
Has driven away through an arch of palms.

The driver finds his eyes in the rearview mirror
Like opals, adjusts his cap, undoes his tie.

Now I have paced your narrow front walk
Glanced at the pansies, the geraniums in your yard,

Mounting the three unpainted steps of your porch
I reach the screen door of your memory:

Cease to resist,
This bed here, this belongs to me

*

And the shore onto which I am about to step

## CARAVAGGIO: THE PAINTING OF FORCE AND VIOLENCE

**I**

Abraham's thumb digs into Isaac's jaw.
Like all Caravaggio's victims Isaac howls.
Of course he is terrified,
The teeth show, the eyes bug out, pushed
Into our faces inviting us to see
What it must mean to be obsessed and shameless.

Surprise is part of it, a father's
Kitchen knife at our peachy throat, the father's
Forearm restrained by the angel who has
Hastily but firmly appeared on the canvas' left margin.

Abraham has forced his head round, looks annoyed
At the interruption, as if he might shake off the hand's pressure
In another instant, and at the right
The profile of a comically stupid white goat,
Almost more pasted than painted,
Peers curiously at the entire scene—

This is a test—are you the boy, or the vigorous
Old father, or the well-bred angel, or the goat?

Do you place yourself in the hands of the living God?

**II**

The inner life holds no interest
For an art not of silence but clamor

The man is a gambler a lecher a drunkard a brawler
A man without delicacy who has "ruined the art of painting . . ."

"Works for a fortnight then enjoys himself for a month . . ."
Flaunting a vulgar unheroic Lombard realism
Contemporary to Galileo and a world of solid objects,
The human figure a physical object possessing weight
Solidity balance and surface areas
No more difficult to paint, he boasts, than fruit or flowers.
His unseductive madonnas physical as his cheeky, delicious
Catamite boys,
His shadows like a fist
His light wielded like a shovel
Large, arbitrary and inexplicable
The dirty feet of his peasants in the foreground
Grey-pink, it is always a question of the truth
Truth is always a question of force
To paint the hundred variations of force
The world requires an ignobly modern man
A quick man with a sword
A man who despises Plato.

### III

As a chemist experiments patiently combining
Materials and recording each effect
So he explores violence and forces
Himself into each position out of nothing
But hot fascination, cold skill
A devilish indifference to all
But the unresolved tensions of any act
Immediately prior to a final result
So that Judith performs her job of sawing
Holofernes' head off with a look of disgust and insult
On her housewife's countenance, her aproned upper

Body pulled backward, her arms the arms
Of a competent butcher;
The creased crone on our far right, however,
Strains maliciously forward. *Do it, don't faint*
*Now, young woman, do it! Kill the pig,*
Urges her mean profile, unlike the goat's,
And the drunken general is twisting
His half-decapitated self around to try and tell,
*Che diavolo,* what is happening to him—
Only the blood is unreal
Leaving his neck not in spurts but stripes, like paint.

**IV**

When the giant's head is removed and the body nowhere in sight
When the victor suspends it in air by its own black greasy hair

Still the image conveys no repose, no triumph or calm or ease,
For see how the youth's compressed lips are hardly at rest,

How his foreshortened arm has already begun to ache
So his shoulder will tire soon, he will set the gross head down,

How Goliath's opened mouth has not yet begun to drip
Saliva, nor stunned eyes to admit their loss,

Behold through the broken brow how self repents its past
While David regards the horror his future holds.

## RVR: WORK AND LOVE

Your coach leaps forward like an act of love
From pious Leiden to Amsterdam, where you eye
The action, bankers and beggars, wealth and art,
Fishwives and Jews at market. Your puppy face
Eager for the life of art is pink-and-green
With ambition, innocent of defeat.

Some early paintings hint a fear of defeat
A mournful Tobit with little dog, the busywork
Of Jesus healing, a blinded Samson, the supine chrome
Corpse dissected by Dr. Tulp—but the amber eye
Triumphs, guilders roll in, your rollicking face
Prospers beneath helmets and plumes, as art

Would have it, and what pleasure to make art
Of "the humble, the rough, the decayed," the lame defeated
Whose inner tenderness rises like cream to their faces.
Or is it your own tenderness? What makes you eye
Cottage and marble hall with equal love?
What presses you to draw from shadows a light

Of something half divine, as it were gold
Undimmable in a plowman's purse? and the art
To make *line,* that poorest mark, thoughtfully work
Through flesh like God's compassion, etching defeat
Like "the greatest inward emotion" a clear eye
Can absorb? Then the theater of *Nightwatch.* Then you face

Saskia's death, creditors, the paintbrush slows, your face
Grows plump but humble, ruddiness gone brown
As a muddy millstream, bankrupt, bags for eyes.
Old-fashioned for the times, your darkened art

69

Makes Hendrickje a fat Bathsheba, denies defeat,
Prepares a copperplate. Now what's left to love?

A window, a studio, a man in a smock at work.
Wearied, persistent, finally your face
Reveals your secret: the identity of triumph and defeat,
Pride and humility, profit and loss. Through the black
Crosshatch as you gaze outward from the art-
Work you work on, I see your deathless eyes

Shadowed by trouble, fortified by love,
Looking me in the eye, helping me face
Bravely my own short art and long defeat.

## ASYLUM: COROT AT THE VILLE D'AVRAY

Olive green where a river
Flows warmly in sunlight,

Olive brown where an oak shadow
Falls across the flow,

Warm dust lightly falling
Half visible in the shade.

A brush laden with forest green
Like icing on a knife

Strokes the estate of the canvas
Forth and back, back and forth.

The river is quiet,
Crows populate the far foliage,

Beyond those embrasured hills
The painter protects you.

## HOMAGE TO REDON

Blurred outlines and shadowed dove grays
Like the gesturing finger of a cowled nocturnal guide
Who directs you from the hot, noisy bar,
The sticky stem of the dropped wineglass,
Through unfamiliar unpeopled streets,
Possibly toward a river in whose groin
Glowing streetlamps will be plunged like swords.

Memory coils like cigarette smoke.
A bit of tobacco sticks to your lip.
Once you were nothing special, you floated,
Tendril in jelly, deaf to the gypsies
Camped near the cathedral square.
Acrid, harsh, their *duende*-inflected song,
A guttering candle, a tingling tambourine.

Here is the alley of brown undifferentiation
Where the artists live wickedly,
The buildings damp, the toilets poor.
Here is a sinister card, an invitation.

*Let sight imagine it can perform the work*
*of smell and taste, hearing and ravished touch.*
*Let sight open the wounds of the dream.*

## BONNARD RETROSPECTIVE

What ripe interiors whose wallpapers
Sofas and kitchen tables bleed together
Like the proverbial village of synchronized women

In the primitive world of someone like Gauguin
Or Rousseau, although surely this is France?
What womblike gardens, stifling, vibrant, junglish

Fabrics abuzz, strange purples flicking green
Like acid odors, softness of pear, dryness of knife,
A dangerous lime safety, where are we?

Areas whose colors are merely sketched in,
Whacked over jangling hot others, the brushstrokes
Actually spineless, nothing like Monet's

Brisk rich purposeful economies,
Make a rather disturbing comfort,
And everywhere, tawny, inescapably bathing

The evanescent Marthe, all torso, all shadow,
A servitude that glows like absence
Syruped, raisined and available

Floating across a melancholy orange undercoat,
Are these the mysteries of domestic
Life in the modern void?

Exhausted plenitudes!
Meaning and technique elude our thought
Until in the final room his self-portraits

Shock: he paints himself in the image
Of a mail clerk, a peeled
Onion, chinless, imprurient, effaced.

## COSI FAN TUTTE: OF DESIRE AND DELIGHT

**I    1761–1769**

> I might here take the opportunity of entertaining the public
> with a story such as probably appears but once in a century,
> and which in the domain of music has perhaps never yet
> appeared *in such a degree of the miraculous;* I might describe the
> wonderful genius of my son.
>
> —LEOPOLD MOZART, "Preliminary Notice" to the
> 2nd edition of his *Violinschule,* 1769

Because Desire is a tomcat rubbing up
Against a cook's leg, childhood a chemise
Unlaced to suckle you, boyhood a room

In which your hands discover a complete
Language to entertain yourself and them,
Whose lexicon and syntax seemingly

Lift through the wooden keys and offer touch
To fingertips you offer, let them come
To pleasure Papa too. What is it like

To reach and feel something reach in response,
Desiring your desire to seek and find?
Between your lessons, Papa wants to know.

So! It is like dream-walking in a wood,
Aware that you yourself create stately
Beeches and oaks ahead as you proceed:

You sniff the air, a cuckoo chirps, a leaf
Twirls silver, sunlight splashes between limbs,
An acorn drops, a gold ray strikes your shirt.

When you perceive you have produced that ray,
That oak and cuckoo, from the mind's brown seed,
It humbles you and crams you with a pride

You cannot then forget, cannot reveal
But in the language, gold, articulate,
Already known for certain by your hands.

**II    1789**

> Apart from the fact that at the moment I am not in a position
> to pay you back this sum, my confidence in you is so
> boundless that I dare to implore you to help me out with a
> hundred florins until next week. . . .
>
> —WOLFGANG MOZART to Michael Puchberg, 1788

Because Delight is a vessel upon a sea
Smoothed by a halcyon and immortal breath,
Whose passengers are young, do not know death,

Do not lack coin, manners, or a bright
Confidence in their own enlightenment,
Who love like figures in a gallant dance,

Rolling eyes upward if an elder prates
Of God and duty, for do not the Estates
General proclaim the rights of man, and does not

Civilization without discontent
Prepare itself for fresh prosperity,
Fresh liberty? Wolfgang, my lad, because

Munich and Prague delight to honor you
Yet do not pay well, and because it's true
Papa is dead and life's a masquerade,

Here's a libretto lets you trumpet what
Fidelity and honor signify
Among the crumbling privileged: suspend

Your horns and strings from heaven's fulcrum like
A rope swing with a pretty woman on it
Pushed by a pretty man in hose and wig

Who is untroubled by a father, who
Need not beg florins from inferiors.
Let your drums beat and let your fiddles play

In strict obedience to the sacred laws
Of gravity, levity, of flaxen curls
And skyblue slippers on the buxom girl

Who swings while singing to enchant her friend,
*Architecture is frozen music, and*
*Music itself a palace of melting ice.*

## SCHUMANN, OP. 16: THE GREATER HAPPINESS

On the stage Robert Schumann is getting drunk

With tempestuous love. You remember what it is to listen to passionate
Nineteenth century music, a clamor of argument and struggle
Invoking the old gods, thunderbolt and hurricane,
At the moment of their dying, and here in the lightning
Is Clara whose father forbids her to marry him.

The middle-aged pianist plunges through the keys.

I sit back to savor the performance, then suddenly find myself
Inside a glissando as inside a storm, flooded and windswept,
Then sense on my face an expression of my shy dead father's,
A twitch of ironic rue at the eyebrow, and presently I feel him
Look through my eyes like sea-cave openings, bone binoculars.

The pianist pours his strength into Robert's ferocity.
Somewhere under the hurricane a sea turtle rows through silence.

Thunder sings, fleecy skies shine, and my father can see
The music through my skull's apertures. He is happy for me
That in my life I can wallow in such music, not like his life.
Our family didn't do beauty, we did poverty, his soul aches with regret.
He too might have loved beauty but whatever you miss in this life you miss
forever.

We sit together, my face awash in tears, pity for his jocular sneakers, his
union card,
His eyes jealous when I went to college, my mother's pointless tirades,
My useless guilt. A girl who watches her father sink
Under billows of anger must want to escape, but the truth
Is I abandoned him. So I praise God

That the roads between the worlds are open again,
Then he says to my soul, not in words, *Tell your mother I love her.*
And my soul is still more happy sitting in the velvet seat in the front
    orchestra
Following the cadenza like an engine of tears, like a wet silence, arpeggios
Trembling in every direction, *He loves her, he always loved her,* the wave

That overwhelms us is only a portion of ocean, what flooded my parents
    was just
Thirty years of tragic human love, like between Robert and Clara,
Like all passion when the gods are still alive,
And somewhere under the hurricane a sea turtle rows through silence,
Somewhere my father rocks asleep on the wave.

Modern, modern, modern—
In the middle of the first
Movement I decide
Janacek is like Chagall
Although Janacek has no
Curved lines and Chagall
No straight ones. Certain
Hot genes must have
Seared Eastern Europe,
Spread like thornfire
Over steppes, stalking into cities
Wearing the cloak
Of plaintiveness and irony
(Black gabardine, red satin lining)
Straitly curved. The cellist,
Oldest of the quartet, seems
Faintly demonic, a troll
Or leprechaun, the first violinist
A sulky muscular bull,
The second violin a romantic
In his forties, a Jewish Afro,
The viola a grown altar boy
Or a chess geek. These four
Bourgeois, they *are* the music
While the music lasts.
            It is the moment
Of the death of God
And the splintering of empire,
Flesh and wit set briefly free,
Nude elbows on a boulevard
Lined with jewelry emporia,

Cafés of mirrors, flowers,
Tubercular lovers. Oh,
Janacek, what a brace
Of hope-besotted ironists
You modern geniuses were.

## RAVEL PIANO TRIO

Suppose I am a starving doe on your lawn.
Do you say *too many deer,* and go for a gun?

Do you play Ravel's Piano Trio in A minor for me
Breathing its hints of diamond moonlit meadows?

Do you throw me food with your own
Nail-bitten agitated hand?

## THE FAURÉ REQUIEM

The flat field of your chest
Stretches like a drumskin

Once there was a seabed here
Then a swamp, the shells and fossils

Lie crushed in their burgeoning forms
No longer crazily trying to breathe

No longer calling out for help
And a deer steps toward you, a beauty

Oblivious to anxiety, she treads
Lightly across your chest,

Pauses, her head turns
On the utterly graceful neck,

Her gaze falls through your eyes
While the pain sharpens

It says something
Always must die

And you would like to remain
Held in that gaze, motionless

Unquestioning, letting whatever
Is going to happen, happen.

It is late afternoon, the cherries bloom.
The master returns to his hillside pavilion
After a great absence.
Donkey trots him over bridge,
Burdened servant follows with lantern,
A child runs up stone steps from the river
Carrying two jars,
A dog comes forth to meet the master.

On a pole a banner
Shows how the wind blows.
And this is all on silk.

Foreground cliffs, bristling pines for tongues,
Argue for nature's solidity, while a background
Mountain half in mist argues against
This and many other illusions.
Tree-limbs, rocks, river, bridge, pavilion.
Browns, greens, washes and accents.
Tiny pink stipples—
Cherry trees blooming in both the worlds.

*

Early fall, the maples auburn,
The cart driver crossing the ford
Whistles to his bullocks.
Is he not a secret philosopher,
Lover of the countryside,
Of solitude and hard work,
Such as holds a land together,
Keeping peace among clans?

84

When nothing else is required of them
Reeds doze, fish conceal themselves,
Willows tremblingly wait to be noticed.
Space seeps back like a banished prince
To his own kingdom:
Change, law, energy, presence.

\*

The pathway of the sages climbs the mountain.
As it approaches heaven,
The mountain itself is tugged at the taproot
By the entry of the artisan.

Now the path pauses at a shelter
Beneath hemlocks,
Now rises through a drift
Of moistened atmosphere.

To what should we compare the boundless forests?
They are like a swell of music
When the musicians are sober
And the patrons ecstatic.

The mountain is like a bell
That chimes extremely softly as the artisan
Unbuttons his quilted vest, cocking his head,
Setting down his cup and bowl.

# IV · TEARING THE POEM UP

## SQUIRRELS

The rodent family, and therefore an enemy,
But, like rabbits, supposedly loveable,

Thanks to cuteness; which consists, apparently,
In a fluffy, as opposed to a ratlike, tail.

Or perhaps our urban migrations have left us wanting
Some animal we can register as charming;

View in parks; condescend to without understanding;
Probably a late nineteenth or an early

Twentieth century form of sentiment; ask
A historian or a sociologist (and remember

The great Parisian cat massacre, or the use
Of monkeys for food in China: one buys them

In baskets hung outside a shop, which the traveler
May mistake for a pet shop, often they're lame);

Pests nonetheless; diseased; mean; capable
Of conquering any bird feeder, by sheer

Concentrated persistence, daring leaps,
Trembling intensity. Like certain shrewd

Politicians, compared with whom we lack—
Apparently—the requisite conviction.

# A WALKER IN THE CITY

What you see is what you get,
An inventory of garbage lying loose—
The poor are always with us, but the rich
Lurk behind one-way glass in limousines
And an entire class of attractive youth
Increasingly able to make money
Without actually working
Increasingly are into arts and leisure.

There's power and there's glamour and there's grief,
That's what a city is for, it's why we come,
There's violence more or less unchanged
Apart from a brief spike on nine-one-one.

The movies and TV are minting it.
Maybe the city should publish maps
Showing the areas of greatest crime
For the benefit of the interested tourist
With special blue stars for locations
Of especially famous crimes, the way in London
Two shillings lets you follow the career
Of Jack the Ripper with a little booklet.

Midtown East Side, here's where Robert Chambers
Strangled his pretty girlfriend during sex
In Central Park. Up by the reservoir
Someone from lower Harlem jumped and raped
And beat for kicks, get it, a woman jogger
Into not death but coma. We thought it was
Five boys, but that was wrong. Running between
A playground and a lake, Strawberry Fields,

Some blackbirds in the shady sycamores
Mark where across the street on 72nd
The Beatles fan Mark Chapman killed John Lennon.
*Imagine there's no heaven, and imagine*
*The people living in a world of peace.*
You have to take the A train to see where
Bernie Goetz pulled out his .44
And stopped the boy he thought another mugger
From sneering with his friends, from making fun.
They come on with their nasty stares, unlaced,
It's so hard to be white, to be a man,
When black kids don't respect you. Here's Howard Beach,
Another white on black question of turf
And goodbye Yusef Hawkins. Here's where the woman guard
In the parking garage got herself shot
Between bright eyes for being eyewitness
To some drug dealer's murder. Here a Bronx housewife
Weary of scrubbing cracked linoleum
Trying to clean her street of crack, lost it,
And the proud Haitian in his candy store the same,
As he wiped his hands on his apron,
And half a dozen children caught in crossfire
One steamy week in summer. *Mama, mama*
*Ayudame, no puedo*—Here's the house
Where Joel Steinberg hit his little daughter
For pleasure, or for anger, breaking bone
After bone, yanking the soft blond curls
While the mom cowered in her druggie daze.
The case is special because he was a lawyer
And had a lot of money, otherwise it wouldn't count.
It wouldn't count. And in this very courtyard

Of comfortable brick and stone
Kitty Genovese, mother of them all,
Ushering in an era,
Screamed, in 1960, being stabbed
Several times in the chest by her old boyfriend,
*Help me! Somebody help me!*
None of the neighbors who heard that woman scream
For an entire hour called the police,
A sensible restraint, all things considered.
That was the sort of thing that shocked us then.

It is important to keep the selection of crimes
Racially balanced and symmetrical
For tourist purposes, as the mayor says.
Right now everyone seems worried
About black people killing white people.
That's the disturbing thought if you are white,
Though naturally most of the people killed
Are men of color. There could be a key
At the map's bottom explaining what was what
If you are here on a self-guided tour.
Maybe the sponsors of the map could be
The NRA, and maybe they'd agree
To have an advertisement on the back,
Like flower shops and banks in highschool yearbooks.

We'd need another color code to show
Where most nonviolent crimes have taken place,
Wall Street, City Hall, Police Headquarters, The Board
Of Education (Bored of Ed) and Columbia University.
Some people rob you with a knife

Some with a fountain pen
Some with an IBM.
And a map to show the areas
Of crimes of omission?
Color the whole map red.
Color the city red.
Color it ghost white
For the death of compassion.

## A VOICE AT THE RALLY

At fourteen I didn't want to be a demonstrator,
I wanted to be a sorority sister.
By the time I was eighteen
Public opinion had changed,
First thing I read in the paper
Was the obituaries.
I had a boyfriend in Nam
And let me tell you there were no *outside agitators*
Bringing me out. I was there.
The day after Nixon called protestors bums
And the governor of Ohio said we were worse
Than brownshirts and Klansmen,
Inciting guardsmen to see kids
Like me
Who just opposed the war
As *the most militant well-trained group ever*
*Assembled in America,*
Was the day it happened.
Four dead in Ohio, not just a song.
I have no forgiveness for the men who faced us
With fixed bayonets and hatred in their eyes.
It's twenty years and I'm still bitter.


*Kent State, Ohio, May 1990*

## THREE WOMEN

*—for Gigliola Sacerdoti*

I

For me it is like a series of slides,
The summer of 1943.
I was almost five,
Our family had gone to the beach,
Too poor to flee to Palestine,
When the deportations began.
We lived with a peasant family
As if we were their relatives,
They must have been brave
Though of course they were paid.
I saw lambs being born
And sheep killed.
The farmer taught my father to skin them.
Germans came to the front door,
Partisans to the back,
I was equally afraid of both.
The partisans needed mattresses in the woods
For the wounded, they said.
We had double mattresses so my father
Took one from each bed
And when he took mine I cried and cried.
One night the peasants told us to leave,
We were in danger,
They had dug a hole in the earth for us
In the middle of the forest.
Nobody explained it to me but
I remember the silent packing.
My mother put on the yellow dress she knitted
For me inside out and didn't listen

When I cried and cried.
All night we hid in the hole.
In the middle of the night was noise.
My mother clamped her hand over my mouth.
It was the Nazis marching over us.

## II

When the camp was liberated some of us teenage girls
ran away. We were a group of perhaps thirty. We
discovered in the forest a deserted German house, like in
a fairy tale. Very fine although full of cobwebs. Not a
farmhouse but a "country" house with tall ceilings and
large bathrooms, so the people must have been well-off.
A gilded mirror hung in the hall and I went up to it
immediately, wanting to see what I looked like now. I
pushed my way through the crowd of hungry girls. And
then, you know, it was too frightening, none of the faces
in the glass was me. For a moment I thought: did I really
die? By sticking out my tongue like a small child, I
learned which of the faces was me. But it remained a
stranger.

## III

Barbed wire higher than I ever saw.
As I looked around I said to myself
If there's a hell on earth, this is it.

One day when we were walking
A woman in line jumped out and started shouting
Children! Children! Of course she wanted to know

About her own child. At that moment the SS
Let go of the two German shepherds
And they tore her to bits.

Mengele was an
Extremely good-looking, very well polished
Elegant German officer,

A kind-looking face, almost like an angel.
The only thing that betrayed his soul
was the look in his eyes, of a devil.

Our barrack next to the crematoria,
Every day we saw the bodies,
The flames shooting up.

We believed if we kept silent
It might make the memories go away,
But they constantly come back.

They stab me,
I don't understand why,
But they obtrude on me. So now I speak.

## THE OTHELLO SARABANDE, OR: THE OCCUPATION

*—for Jim Council and Mary Campbell*

My occupation's love; it's nothing else.
                —St. John of the Cross

Othello's occupation's gone.
                —*Othello*, III.3

Othello's occupation was gone when he believed her a magpie that could
    fly from tree
To tree after he had fought to build a nest, a fine nest to contain her
    beauty, and with a flurry
Of noble song fought off her father, and we cannot say whether this
    occupation was love
Or war, perhaps he confused them, his was a simple soul,

A young and innocent soul, in the clothing of a seasoned soldier. We of
    mankind,
We humans, we sapiens, we for whom knowledge is a lens and a
    blindfold,
Yearn to possess what we love, to love what we possess,
And there's always a war, always the tree that is the body

With the nest that holds the spirit, always the fear
That the spirit will blow where it listeth, and if so, then what will become
Of me? the self that's left? Iago is that fear, true love casts out fear,
    Othello's love
Therefore isn't perfect, and when our love isn't perfect

We want to kill the thing we love, that's the thing with a young soul, it
    behaves like a child.
Desdemona is the Christ figure who pities him, rejoices him, appeals to
    his goodness,

Dies for him. Her innocence is different, hers is an old (that is wise)
 soul. We are shown
Maps of love and hate, an array of loves and hates, we are asked to enjoy
 the show.

Or Desdemona is Gaia, and dies for Othello after singing a song about a
 willow tree,
Folk song whose notes gently cascade from unremembered time
When we praised and honored spirit-containing trees—
Dies unprotesting, for the earth has no voice that we understand.

No voice that we understand. Or Desdemona is Jerusalem, the city who
 sits and weeps
Is any sorrow like my sorrow, her blood is in her skirts, her lovers call her
 whore
The rest is silence and I wonder whether Desdemona's pain is mitigated
 by any sense
That Othello has learned something. That her sacrifice has been of use.

The curtain falls and then the curtain falls.
Do I not want to kill what I cannot possess?
Is it not the task of poets to raise the mirror to the world's face, to say lo
 and behold,
See here, will you just look at yourself, the occupation is love, the rest is
 silence?

The death of a beautiful woman is beautiful.
Put out the light and then put out the light.
Desdemona is gone, Jerusalem will be arrayed as a bride,
Gaia is a prisoner, all poems ask who will free her.

The poem is not a possession, it is a door
Through which we pass from our greedy world to the world
Where there is no possessing nor possession
And live there until we close the book.

## ELEGY FOR ALLEN

That was a break
In the fiber of things
Sorrowful
When Ginsberg died
Because I still have students
Wanting to be Beats
And even some
Wanting to be Buddhists
Why not, but when
That brilliant Jew poet took
The train for the next world
American nirvana
Temporarily went with him.
Not that he ever attained
The tranquility
Supposedly sought,
He was so nervous
And somehow ailing,
The neurotic utopian
Prophetic fairy side
Of the guy never
Surrendered really
To those Asian things
And too much ginseng
Makes a man feeble-like.
Yes, B— says
You would be there
At a party and he'd say
Excuse me I have to follow
That young man, you'd think
Fine but why are you obliged

To announce it, why not
Just do it.

The greatest Jewish poet
After Celan and Amichai,
I cry, grieving, and
B— says better not try
To sell him as a rabbi
Though what else is he
For heaven's sake
Beads and bells
And dreams of peace
And all.

## TEARING THE POEM UP AND EATING IT

> You shall not oppress a stranger; for you know the heart
> of the stranger, for you were strangers in Egypt.
>
> —EXODUS 23:9

> And they shall beat their swords into ploughshares.
>
> —ISAIAH 2.4

*—in memory of Yitzhak Rabin*

**I**

Take this, they said
Handing it to me
As if I were a prophet or a wise woman
As if a poem were something healing
As if a poem nourished
Not only itself, the life of language
Which certainly is worth nothing
Next to a biological life—
*What are you saying?*
*Do you think the life of an insect*
*Is worth more than the life of a poem?*

In childhood I did—
That is exactly what I thought
An ant, a pink-grey worm on the wet sidewalk
Was worth everything.

**II**

Dear God: my people say
Your justice is like rain
They also call you a compassionate God
So that I try to believe

Justice and compassion together
Pour through the lifeblood of your poem,
Your book, but tell it to the bloody plaza
Tell it to the stone of sacrifice
Where the sons finally rise to slay the father
Tell it to the assassin's rabbi and his grandmother
Speak the poem to her oranges and fish.

### III

Numb before the drama of the television
I watch them annihilate words like *ploughshare.*
I walk the boulevard of middle eastern history
Where everything looks familiar, I watch
Zeal like a tough many-legged insect
Pestiferous, running and biting, indestructible
Ecstasy pressing the tender trigger,

Hope like a manhole the clown falls into,
Wind of the spirit flows toward the aperture
Like gnats pouring into throats of birds,
A man like a pink-grey worm on the sidewalk,
Compassion and justice like raped girls after a party
Of whom one asks, What were they drinking,
Why did they dress in skirts so short?

—Tearing the poem up and eating it
Will get me nowhere. Better to burn than to marry
What demands to be married, what offers its ring
Of spurious safety, what demands that I sell my birthright
Of hope and forget to remember the heart of the stranger

And better to write than to burn
And best to clear a path for the wind.

IV

At the funeral one of the ministers produced
What will obviously be the icon of this martyrdom:
The sheet of paper bearing the words of the peace song
He sang at the rally ten minutes before his assassination
The paper was folded into quarters and stained
With an irregular shape of blood from where
It was in his pocket, fire and blood

You wonder at funerals why nobody bursts out laughing

His granddaughter touchingly said to the microphone that she
Knew angels would bear him to heaven and perhaps they will, who
Am I
To doubt

V

The rabbi said to his son:
I will give you ten gold coins
If you can tell me where God is
The boy answered:
I will give you twenty
If you can tell me where he is not

The moral:
If blood still stains the paper
It is God's blood,
Is it not?

## VI

Yet those who believe you chose them
    break the bones of the unchosen
Those who trust in your righteousness
    study death's secret handshake
Those who remember you promised them the land
    sow it with corpses
Those who await messiah
    dream of apocalypse
    in which their enemies burn—
I speak of all your countries, my dear God.

## DIVREI

At Masada we gave you our souls
At Auschwitz we took them back
We learned to defend ourselves
We repeated *Never again* and taught it to our children
We built our bodies

Oh you who have countless eyes
Whose entire body is eyes, eyes and language
You who say *Not by might and not by power*
Will you stop dreaming, my God
Do you understand nothing?

# FIX

The puzzled ones, the Americans, go through their lives
Buying what they are told to buy,
Pursuing their love affairs with the automobile,

Baseball and football, romance and beauty,
Enthusiastic as trained seals, going into debt, struggling—
True believers in liberty, and also security,

And of course sex—cheating on each other
For the most part only a little, mostly avoiding violence
Except at a vast blue distance, as between bombsight and earth,

Or on the violent screen, which they adore.
Those who are not Americans think Americans are happy
Because they are so filthy rich, but not so,

They are mostly puzzled and at a loss
As if someone pulled the floor out from under them,
They'd like to believe in God, or something, and they do try.

You can see it in their white faces at the supermarket and the gas station
—Not the immigrant faces, they know what they want,
Not the blacks, whose faces are hurt and proud—

The white faces, lipsticked, shaven, we do try
To keep smiling, for when we're smiling, the whole world
Smiles with us, but we feel we've lost

That loving feeling. Clouds ride by above us,
Rivers flow, toilets work, traffic lights work, barring floods, fires
And earthquakes, houses and streets appear stable,

So what is it, this moon-shaped blankness?
What the hell is it? America is perplexed.
We would fix it if we knew what was broken.

# THE WINDOW, AT THE MOMENT OF FLAME

And all this while I have been playing with toys
A toy power station a toy automobile a house of blocks

And all this while far off in other lands
Thousands and thousands, millions and millions—

You know—you see the pictures
Women carrying their bony infants

Men sobbing over graves
Buildings sculpted by explosion

Earth wasted bare and rotten—
And all this while I have been shopping, I have

Been let us say free
And do they hate me for it

Do they hate *me*

## FROM THE MOON

Our excellence will be so obvious,
More precious than jewels, this bright
Blue-and-green marble
With its moveable pallors
Will speak to the hand and eye
Its mute discourse of beauty—

Any boy would want it
For a possession of his
Own, to cup in his palm and carry
In his pocket, like a favorite knife—

Heartbreakingly poignant, the way
The phrase *this England* used to sound
With its meaning of *separate island,*
Or the way *God bless America*
Was an actual prayer, that is to say a wish,
Fragrant and green—the sight will be
Both paradise recalled, and a taste
Of perfect misery.

They will look at us then,
From afar, hopelessly in love,
They will gaze at our great grave.

## POEM SIXTY YEARS AFTER AUSCHWITZ

*—for C. K. Williams*

On a day of marching, the police in London
Were bored and benign, not needing to keep order
For the million marching people were orderly.

Although they came from around the world,
They were mostly Englishmen and Englishwomen,
Many carried signs saying "Make Tea Not War."

Horses stood motionless, questioned why they were not
Allowed to move, and from time to time would shake
Their glossy bodies impatiently. The marchers flowed over London

Bridge, flowed past Nelson remotely on his pillar,
Past Whitehall, past Green Park to Hyde Park, traffic was banned,
People were drops of water composing a river

And their signs and posters were a writing taken off the wall
And made into sails, what a beautiful clear cold day.
A day for sailing, a day for reading the signs.

I did not know life would inspire so many
To come out in its favor, patiently marching,
Singing the occasional song. On the same day

In New York the marching permit was withheld
So the people and the police struggled,
Forming whirlpools and dams, areas of dangerous turbulence,

Some scowling mounted officers charged the crowd, let the
Horses rear. There were other cities, Rome, Madrid, Mexico City
—And the weather was cold, or it was warm—

Dozens of cities, people marching
Like sands of the sea and stars of the sky,
Or like stems of snowdrops nudging the frozen dirt

Piled on their heads, unburying themselves
Before it's officially springtime, here's a patch by the brick wall
Next to our garage that I look up from my book to see,

Glowing white and brave, a little afraid, a little aware
Of the brevity of their visit here. It happens that
The book I'm reading is *Poetry after Auschwitz*

And I set it down after learning of a poem describing how
From a mass grave a fountain of blood spurting up
Surprised even the officer in charge.

This is one of a thousand interesting stories the book tells,
For poems after the holocaust remember, or imagine,
How sick and sickening people can become,

And now I think we are writing the poems before the holocaust.
Is this not true? We are writing these poems with all our soul,
It's our writing, it's our wall.

# HUNGER

**I**

It was 1913 and there was no money.
She was born a runt who vomited everything,
So much poverty, such thin milk,
The doctor said to let her go in the dark
And have another child when there was money for food
But her mother persisted, insisted,
For months feeding and feeding
The skin on bones until she lived and grew,

But still remembers hunger, even now
Shaking her soft white hair,
She remembers hunger and vomiting,
Remembers seeing her mother approach with the bottle,
Her desperate need to suck and be filled,
And at the same instant the grip of despair. And the force of will.

**II**

She remembers also the dresses her mother sewed her,
Woolen, tucked, pleated, exceptional,
In dead European styles that made her ashamed
When she went to school, which insulted her mother,

But anyway, her mother never loved her
After that hard beginning. Fix your hair,
My grandma was still scolding in the wheelchair
Whenever my poor mother visited

The Workman's Circle Home for the Aged.
Fix your hair, she would say, grimacing,
And reach to fix it, and my mom got rashes,
My mom got asthma before each visit.

**III**

They fired my father, they thought he was a Commie,
And it was still the Depression when I was born.
She remembers how she tied my arms and legs to the highchair
So that I wouldn't flail and she could get the spoon in
Though she and my father were hungry.
She told that one to my school counselor,
Boasting, and the counselor told me
To separate from my mother,
That she was crazy.

*I wanted to be the best mother in the world,*
She says in a voice like hoarded string.
*That was what I wanted, but I failed.*
Here I freeze as always, and swallow my spit.
*I failed, but I did my best.*

As a girl she was a wild one, a *vilde chaia,*
She says into the little microphone
I hold for her as the casette whirs on.
She beat up a boy on her block who cheated at cards,
She refused to be tidy, she ran away from home.

We stand to go to the dining room, where because
The meal is free she will stuff herself as if
She were still that infant, she'll eat her own ice cream
And mine, she'll tell her neighbor that I
Am her sun and moon and stars,
And before I leave she will hug me
As if we were lovers.

**IV**

And I too had my dreams of improvement and perfection.
I too hungered to give abundant life to my children.

## ELEGY BEFORE THE WAR

**I**

All the photographs are lies, she looks
Normal in them, like other people,
Not mad, not spilling lava,

Her eyes are compelling as does' eyes,
And she did not know this, and the worst of it is
She looks alive.

Putting the photos away, I also picture
How small and frightened she was in the hospice bed,
How light abandoned the hopeful gaze,

How the mouth gap with its gurgle from the sad
Lungs made us feel like Moses, made to see
God's backside from a cleft in the rock,

The mystery diminished not one grain,
The face and hands outside the cotton quilt
Soft, horrible, fine—

How the jaw tightened then fell open
Almost with a bang, the aide nodded,
Everyone left, and then there was her silence,

A silence in which I stroked her moist forehead
Then patted through the nightgown her belly and breasts.
O I loved her and this was her response—

I keep telling her to come back sometime.
Come back! I am not ready
To surrender hope.

II
My mother is dead two weeks

We were holding her hands and singing to her
When she let go. Very little pain, lucid
Almost to the end, correcting
People's grammar
A week before
She died—

And we burned her and flew to Arizona
And the tanks roamed Ramallah and Nablus

I feel as if anything I have to say needs to be shaved down. I want my
    language to be like
The desert. My words and phrases to be like ocotillo, yucca, saguaro.
    Prickly. Thorny.
Able to collect moisture enough to survive extended drought.

The air I breathe is materially tropical, spiritually arid. These are dry
    times, orphan times,
Fear on the wind, anger in the soil. I cannot imagine an appealing future
    for my species,
Born to violence that steers the intelligence.

The air I breathe you breathe.
Just now a molecule breathed by the Buddha
Might have entered your lungs.

Where is Shelley when we need him?
"An old, mad, blind, despised and dying king,
Nobles, the dregs of their dull race,"

He begins a sonnet after the Manchester riots in which
British soldiers shot their fellow citizens dead.
Where is William Blake, is he burning

Bright as the tiger in some grassy meadow of paradise,
Does he beat a drum and shout "Holy holy holy
Is the Lord God almighty," or, on alternate days,

"Exuberance is beauty," and where is Walt Whitman
And where is Ginsberg, genius of kindness?
I beg my mother come back sometime.

The root system of the saguaro
spreads shallowly underground as widely as
the cactus is high.

That of the ocotillo plunges.
The tanks roll, the missiles fly.

Greedy teeth smile at the microphone.
They know where the oil is. They have plans, big plans
To connect the imperial dots.

I beg you awesome ones lift yourselves off the page, be with us
Blow through us like a hot desert wind, as if we were trumpets
As if we were saxophones. Beat on our membranes hard

And let us be drums. Artillery
Will always outshout us, testosterone explosions
Are more thrilling than anything, chain reactions

Brilliance between opposite poles accelerating
At the speed of hate, we do this
To you because

You did it to us first. Thrilling!
The bus explodes,

The shelled house collapses over the grandmother
And the gasping family, the tanks roll, the missiles fly

And perhaps the faster one dies,
The better.

*

But it does explain something.

I too look at the images

Of cruel death in the newspaper and on the screen.
They taste good, I like them. You like them. They are their own
Best advertisement. We like to shudder at them. We like to blame.

We bravely deplore. We enjoy a bit of fury.
The nearer we get to death, the more
We feel alive.

War, that great stimulant,
Let us drink to it.
Let us join our friends, Israel and Palestine.

Our friends who have been seduced by it.

## III

Now that it is spring I open the window at night

I lie awake in my cave, my well of night
Pulsing like a bat
Making inaudible orphan sounds

Though the blinds stay down
Soft air seeps in, a few cars
Swish along the street

From the next house
Where gloomy faded shingles fall like leaves
And bedsheets hang in the windows instead of drapes,

I hear the man's chronic unstoppable cough,
A poor man's cough, and the wife's hoarse voice
Coaxing their dog.

*Gypsy. Stop it. Come here.*
*Good girl, good girl.*
I can work on

Making music of that.

## IV

Where is Auden now? Is he attempting to rejoice?
Is he happy that all he had was a voice?
Does he engage Merrill in contests of puns,
Over in the heaven of the deserving ones?

## V

Friday night getting smashed in America

Ignorant violence that stuns the intelligence.
Dear animal inside us whom in other respects
We cherish, is it you?

Whitman and Blake inside us, celebrants of war equally with peace, is
    it you?
Descendants of Homer? Is it our stars? Is it our cold reason?
Is there a devil? Will somebody pass me that bourbon?

I think this impulse to destroy
This need for an enemy
Has actually nothing to do with sex,

It is simply a human characteristic
It has climbed the corporate ladder of the DNA
It is on the board of directors.

A joke in the Soviet Union went like this:
Under capitalism man is a wolf to man.
Under Communism it's just the opposite.

And there was that other one, about the economy:
We pretend to work, and they pretend to pay us.
Very funny, but because of low morale

The Russians have become ineffective soldiers
Like the Italians and the French.
Long live the Italian and French armies!

Long live the citizens of Prague
Whose twelfth century buildings stand
Because a Czech will fight to the last

Drop of ink! The trouble with America
Is that her morale is still too high.
She needs to be a bit more depressed

Before she starts behaving better.
The trouble with America
Is she is a big bully

And a big coward,
Also that she has no conscience,
Not enough cynics, they are all in Europe.

Now let someone discreetly put on
The Stones or The Doors or better yet
Jimi doing the Star Spangled Banner

Like a cry of absolutely
Pained rage, a train jumping the tracks.
I like this party.

Perhaps you on the other hand like ignorant violence that stunts,
Stints, stains, struts, standardizes, brutally strangles
The intelligence. Somebody must, why not you? Well,

Here we need a few anti-American jokes.
What are we afraid of?
Where are the comedians

When we need them?
Tucked in their cages
Like tame monkeys.

Where are the accountants?
Who will save us
From the mudslide of dollars?

## VI

Blessed be the watercolorists
Who do normal mediocre meadows and lakes
As if the twentieth century never occurred
And blessed be whoever buys their paintings.

## VII

She cried when she read Shakespeare

When I was young, she taught me not to hit or hate
Anybody, she thought education was the answer, she said most people
Were ignorant and superstitious but not us.

I miss her hugs though they were like clamps,
I miss her voice though she often mysteriously screamed
With rage at us all, the shopkeepers, the neighbors.

What drove her crazy, what wasted her beauty and intellect, was it
    America,
The *goldene medina* just a joke, land of bankers and lynch mobs
In her girlhood, land of brokers and bombs at her death,

Hammer to which everything is a nail?

Or was it her pretty mother with the golden voice
And the golden hands that could sew anything
Not loving her enough, the way she claimed?

Or was it a tricky couple of cells?
Little magicians sawing the woman in half?
My mother's secrets die with her,

The obsession with germs
The obsession with money
The anger at the world for cheating her.

Where did she go, my hopeful young mother,
My mother who promised we would overcome
The bosses and bigots? I want her. I want her

To come back and try again.


*April 2002—February 2003*

## DAFFODILS

*—for David Lehman*

Ten thousand saw I at a glance
Tossing their heads in sprightly dance.
    —WILLIAM WORDSWORTH

Going into hell so many times tears it
Which explains poetry.
    —JACK SPICER

The day the war against Iraq begins
I'm photographing the yellow daffodils
With their outstretched arms and ruffled cups
Blowing in the wind of Jesus Green

Edging the lush grassy moving river
Along with the swans and ducks
Under a soft March Cambridge sky
Embellishing the earth like a hand

Starting to illustrate a children's book
Where people in light clothes come out
To play, to frisk and run about
With their lovers, friends, animals, and children

As down every stony back road of history
They've always done in the peaceful springs
—Which in a sense is also hell because
The daffodils do look as if they dance

And make some of us in the park want to dance
And breathe deeply and I know that
Being able to eat and incorporate beauty like this
I am privileged and by that token can

Taste pain, roll it on my tongue, it's good
The cruel wars are good the stupidity is good,
The primates hiding in their caves are very good,
They do their best, which explains poetry.

What explains poetry is that life is hard
But better than the alternatives,
The no and the nothing. Look at this light
And color, a splash of brilliant yellow

Punctuating an emerald text, white swans
And mottled brown ducks floating quietly along
Whole and alive, like an untorn language
That lacks nothing, that excludes

Nothing. Period. Don't you think
It is our business to defend it
Even the day our masters start a war?
To defend the day we see the daffodils?

# CODA

## CODA: INTO THE STREET

*for Gerald Stern*

Here comes the sun again
Reminding everyone to rise and shine
So we pour the coffee and hear the news,

We pick up the paper and sigh like arthritic dogs,
And we might like to blow our exasperated
Brains out, when we think about the world,

Then again we might laugh ourselves silly,
Figure out how to profit by it
Or wonder how to love it anyway,

This is what freedom and consciousness are for,
As if we are standing on the roof
Of a very tall tower

Looking at the complicated view,
Then taking the elevator,
Going out into the street,

Lucky us.

"Running Out the Clock": The quotations are Ecclesiastes 9.10 and 1.8, and H.D.,"The Flowering of the Rod" 2, *Trilogy*.

"Extended Sonnet": The quotation is from a song by Goethe.

*A Material Density*: Many of the paintings in this section can be found online.

"Wooden Virgin with Child": this 13th century sculpture is in the Cloisters, a branch of the Metropolitan Museum of Art in New York City.

"The Kiss of Judas": The Scrovegni Chapel, frescoed by Giotto, is in Padua.

"The Birth of Venus": Botticelli's painting is in the Uffizi Gallery in Florence. The "huge shell" derives from the body of the Babylonian sea goddess Tiamat, whose son killed her and split her corpse in two to make the earth and sky.

"Caravaggio: The Painting of Force and Violence": The three paintings mentioned here are *The Sacrifice of Isaac, Judith Beheading Holofernes,* and *David with the Head of Goliath.*

"RVR: Work and Love": The etching described at the end of the poem, *Rembrandt Drawing at a Window,* was exhibited at the Pierpont Morgan Library in New York City in 2000.

"Bonnard Retrospective": Based on a Bonnard exhibit at the Museum of Modern Art in New York City in 1998.

"A Walker in the City": The NRA is the National Rifle Association.

"Tearing the Poem Up and Eating It": Yitzhak Rabin, Prime Minister of Israel and co-winner of the Nobel Peace Prize in 1994, was assassinated on November 4, 1995, by a Jewish law student who believed Rabin was "giving the country to the Arabs" and said he was acting on the "orders of God." Commandments not to oppress the stranger are repeated a dozen times in various forms in the Hebrew Bible.

"Divrei": lit., "words"; a term used in Talmud to denote contrary arguments. Jews who fled to the desert fortress of Masada after refusing to worship Roman gods killed themselves and their children following a two year siege, in A.D. 73, to avoid capture. Today Masada is an Israeli national shrine and a popular tourist attraction. "Not by might and not by power, but by my spirit," Zechariah 4:6.

"Elegy Before the War": *goldene medina*, "golden land" in Yiddish, immigrants' metaphor for America.

ACKNOWLEDGMENTS

Thanks to the following publications, in which some of the poems
in this collection appeared, some in earlier versions or with
different titles:
*American Poetry Review, American Scholar, Atlantic Monthly, Barrow Street, Bellevue
Literary Review, Columbia, CrossCurrents, 5 AM, Feminist Studies, Inklings, Maggid,
Michigan Quarterly Review, Night Sun, Ontario Review, Pleiades, Prairie Schooner,
Seneca Review, Smartish Pace, Tikkun, Triquarterly Review,* and *Witness.*

"May Rain, Princeton" is reprinted from *Shenandoah: The Washington and
Lee University Review,* with the permission of the editor.

"Hunger" first appeared in *Women's Review of Books.*

"An Album of Chinese Fan Paintings" first appeared in *Double Take,*
Fall 2000.

"Another Imaginary Voyage" first appeared in *Ploughshares* 22.1.

"Correspondence" first appeared in *Columbia: A Journal of Literature and
Art.*

I wish also to express my gratitude to the MacDowell Colony and to
the Bellagio Study and Conference Center for residencies that
enabled me to begin and revise many of these poems, and to
Rutgers University for enabling me to take personal leaves to do so.

Alicia Suskin Ostriker is a poet and critic whose previous volumes of poetry include *The Imaginary Lover* (1986), which won the William Carlos Williams Award of the Poetry Society of America, *The Crack in Everything* (1996), which was a National Book Award finalist and won both the Paterson Poetry Award and the San Francisco State Poetry Center Award, *The Little Space, Poems Selected and New 1968–1998*, also a National Book Award finalist, and, most recently, *the volcano sequence* (2002). Her critical works include *Stealing the Language: The Emergence of Women's Poetry in America* (1986), *The Nakedness of the Fathers: Biblical Visions and Revisions* (1994), and *Dancing at the Devil's Party: Essays on Poetry, Politics, and the Erotic* (2000).